"Big Easy 123" is a delightful children's book that combines the joy of counting with an adventurous exploration of the swamp wildlife. Set in the captivating backdrop of the Louisiana bayous, this story invites young readers to embark on a vibrant journey through nature. As children turn each page, they'll encounter a variety of swamp creatures, from lively alligators and playful frogs to colorful birds and lazy turtles, all while learning to count from one to ten. The book's engaging illustrations and rhythmic text make it an enjoyable read for both kids and parents, inspiring curiosity about the natural world and reinforcing foundational counting skills. Perfect for early learners, "Big Easy 123" is a charming addition to any child's library, blending education with the wonders of the swamp ecosystem.

Also Authors of "ABCs of Mardi Gras"

BIG EASY AS 1 2 3

By April Duplessis Lee
and Marc Lee Sr.

Copyright©2025 by April and Marc Lee Sr.

All rights reserve.

No portion of the book may be reproduced in any form without written permission from the publisher or autho, except as permitted by U.S. copyright law. For permission request, write to the publishe, at the address below:

Ordering Information:

Order by the U.S. trade bookstores and wholesaler. Ouantity sale. Special discounts are available on quantity purchases by corporation, associations, and others. For detail, contact the publisher at the following email address:

Connect with April Duplessis Lee and Marc Lee Sr.
Instagram: nnbooksandtea or lord_of_the_kitchen

Email: thegreenhouse.journey@gmail.com

1 Turtle

2 Alligators

3 Ducks

4 Crickets

5 Snakes

6 Frogs

7 Pelicans

8 Raccoons

9 Otters

10 Owls

1 2 3
4 5 6
7 8 9
10

Made in the USA
Columbia, SC
12 March 2025

55053296R00015